WOMEN'S PROFESSIONAL BASKETBALL

Teamwork:

The

CHARLOTTE STING

in Action

Thomas S. Owens
Diana Star Helmer

The Rosen Publishing Group's
PowerKids Press™
New York

To everyone who has waited or worked for a dream. Here's proof that dreams come true.

Published in 1999 by The Rosen Publishing Group, Inc.
29 East 21st Street, New York, NY 10010

First Edition

Book Design: Michael de Guzman

Photo Credits: p. 4 © Ray Amati/WNBA Enterprises, LLC; pp. 5, 13 © Barry Gossage/WNBA Enterprises, LLC; p. 7 © Reuters/Ray Stubblebine/Archive Photos; p. 8 (left) © Rick Havner/Associated Press, AP, (middle) © Glenn James, (right) © Tim O'Dell/WNBA Enterprises, LLC; p. 11 © Chuck Burton/Associated Press, AP; pp. 12, 16 © Tim O'Dell/WNBA Enterprises, LLC; p. 15 © Rick Havner/Associated Press, AP; p. 19 © Scott Cunningham/WNBA Enterprises, LLC; p. 20 © Andrew Bernstein/WNBA Enterprises, LLC.

Owens, Tom, 1960-
    Teamwork: the Charlotte Sting in action / by Thomas S. Owens and Diana Star Helmer.
        p.   cm. — (Women's professional basketball)
    Includes index.
    Summary: Profiles some of the key players on the Charlotte Sting professional women's basketball team and describes the team's first year in the WNBA.
    ISBN 0-8239-5242-8
    1. Charlotte Sting (Basketball team)—Juvenile literature. 2. Basketball for women—United States—Juvenile literature. [1. Charlotte Sting (Basketball team). 2. Women basketball players. 3. Basketball players] I. Helmer, Diana Star, 1962-   . II. Title.
III. Series: Owens, Tom, 1960-   Women's professional basketball.
GV885.52.C4094 1998
796.323'64'0975676—dc21   98-16493
                                                                                                                      CIP
                                                                                                                      AC

Manufactured in the United States of America

Contents

There's No Place Like Home

At first, when the WNBA's Charlotte Sting played in Charlotte, they won. But when they played in other cities, they lost. Then, halfway through the season, something changed. When Charlotte had to play the Liberty in New York, first Charlotte pulled ahead. Then the Liberty kept scoring points. In the last 1.3 seconds, New York tried to tie the game—but they missed! Charlotte's 64 to 61 proved that they could win wherever they were playing.

The Sting played best at the Charlotte Coliseum. Fans call the Coliseum "the Hive."

5

Sisters of the NBA

The National Basketball Association (NBA) invented the Women's National Basketball Association (WNBA) after the 1996 Olympics. That year, the U.S. Women's Basketball Team won the gold medal. After the Olympics, the team traveled around America to meet their fans. Basketball fans around the country wanted to see these new stars in their own United States basketball **league** (LEEG). WNBA teams play in the same cities as the NBA while the NBA is on summer vacation. The people in Charlotte, North Carolina, were thrilled when they found out that one of the first WNBA teams would be in their city.

The U.S. Women's Basketball Team was thrilled when they beat Brazil to win the 1996 Olympic gold medal. ▶

Old Friends

Even during the Sting's first year, Charlotte fans felt like team members were old friends. And no wonder—Andrea Stinson, Rhonda Mapp, and Sharon Manning had played together for North Carolina State University. Even the college's assistant coach, Karen Freeman, became the Sting's assistant coach.

Andrea and Sharon graduated in 1991. Rhonda graduated in 1992. Then they played **professional** (proh-FEH-shuh-nul) basketball in Europe. Sometimes they were teammates, sometimes they were **opponents** (uh-POH-nents). When the Sting brought them together again, Sharon cheered, "I'd rather play with Rhonda than against her!"

◀ Some Charlotte fans had seen many of the Sting players play college basketball before those players joined the WNBA.

9

A Home Body

Andrea Stinson felt lucky whenever the Sting played at home. To Andrea, Charlotte really is home—she grew up there.

The team felt lucky to have Andrea too. Only four other players in the league scored more points all season. In fifteen Charlotte wins, Andrea scored the most points ten times.

Coach Marynell Meadors says, "I don't think we would have done very well without her. If we can get the ball to her, we know we're going to score."

10

Andrea Stinson is called "Stint" by her ▶
friends, teammates, and coach.

Bullett Proof

Vicky Bullett had to be tough from the minute she was born. It's not just her name that makes her strong. "I was the only girl in the family," she says. "Having six brothers really toughened me up!"

Soon after high school, Vicky played on the 1988 Olympic gold-medal team. Then she played professional basketball in Italy for seven years. She was an All-Star there four times.

Vicky plays tough for the Sting. She was the second-best **shot blocker** (SHOT BLAH-ker) in the WNBA in 1997.

◀ Even with all of her basketball honors, Vicky is most proud of graduating from college.

13

English Made

Andrea Congreaves didn't start playing basketball until she was fifteen years old. Instead she liked track and field. Her father was a track **referee** (reh-fuh-REE). At one meet, he **disqualified** (dis-KWAH-lih-fyd) her twice! But "he was encouraging," Andrea says, especially when she started basketball.

Andrea is from England, where basketball isn't as popular as it is in the United States. She came to the United States to study and play college basketball. Winning awards here, she kept playing for the English National team. In fact, Andrea was late for the first Sting practice because she was playing for England!

14

Coach Marynell Meadors loves the way forward Andrea Congreaves (right) gains control of loose balls and rebounds. ▶

Small Wonder

Nicole Levesque is very small for a basketball player. She is just five feet, three inches tall. Basketball players are usually much taller. But Nicole won awards and played on **championship** (CHAM-pee-un-ship) basketball teams in high school and college. Nicole was not a Charlotte Sting player when the season began. But when a Sting player got hurt, the coach called Nicole. "The coaches have **confidence** (KON-fih-dents) in me and the players believe in me," Levesque says. At the end of the first season, Nicole was one of the WNBA's top twelve players in **assists** (uh-SISTS) and three-point shots.

◀ In college, Nicole Levesque worked during the summers at the basketball camps of famous NBA player Tyrone "Mugsy" Bogues, another great basketball player who isn't very tall.

17

Play On for Play-offs!

    Even after beating New York, the Sting mostly won at home. But they still won more than many teams. At season's end, Charlotte needed just one more win to get to the **play-offs** (PLAY-offs). Luckily, their last game was in the Hive against the Utah Starzz. The Starzz had lost twenty games, and had only won seven. But at **halftime** (HAF-tym), the Starzz were almost tied. They kept playing hard. But the Sting played harder. The Sting won, 70 to 52. Charlotte was going to the play-offs!

The Sting worked their hardest as a team to get to the play-offs. ▶

Leaving the Hive

The first play-off game was against the Houston Comets. And the game was in Houston, not in the Hive. But the Sting was buzzing at the game. If Houston scored, Charlotte scored. The lead went back and forth. The score was tied with nine minutes left.

Suddenly, Houston's Wanda Guyton fell and hit her head. The game stopped. Wanda was carried off the court and taken to the hospital. Charlotte players waited, looking worried. Houston players worried. But Houston's worry turned to energy. When the game started again, Houston played like a new team. And Charlotte lost, 54 to 70.

◀ The Sting tried their best to beat the Comets. Even though they didn't win, they were proud of themselves.

One Year Old

"Although we were excited about making the play-offs in the first WNBA season, we want to win it all next year," Vicky Bullett says. During the off-season, Sting members played around the world to get ready for the second year. Sharon Manning and Andrea Congreaves played in Italy. Vicky Bullett was teammates with Comet Cynthia Cooper in Brazil. Cynthia was the league's 1997 Most Valuable Player (MVP). "I really enjoy playing with Cynthia," Vicky says. Back in North Carolina's Hive, Cynthia and Vicky would be opponents again. But they will still be friends. That's what makes the WNBA fun.

Web Sites:

You can learn more about women's professional basketball at these Web sites:

http://www.wnba.com

http://www.fullcourt.com

Glossary

assist (uh-SIST) Passing the ball to another player so she can score.

championship (CHAM-pee-un-ship) The last game of the season that determines who is the best team.

confidence (KON-fih-dents) A firm belief in oneself and one's abilities.

disqualified (dis-KWAH-lih-fyd) Not allowed to play; or taken out of a game after breaking a rule.

halftime (HAF-tym) A break halfway through a game.

league (LEEG) A group of teams that play against each other in the same sport.

opponent (uh-POH-nent) The team you are playing against.

play-offs (PLAY-offs) A series of games after the regular season that determine who will play in the championship game.

professional (proh-FEH-shuh-nul) Earning money for playing a sport.

referee (reh-fuh-REE) A person who makes sure players follow the rules during a game or sports event.

shot blocker (SHOT BLAH-ker) A person who is able to knock the ball away from the other team as it tries to make a basket.

23

Index